Lessons for the Journey

Watching God move in the everyday lives of everyday people

by

Trey Graham

AmErica House
Baltimore

First printing

ISBN: 1–59129–032–5
PUBLISHED BY AMERICA HOUSE
BOOK PUBLISHERS
www.publishamerica.com
Baltimore

Printed in the United States of America

Dedication

To my God, who always finds
miraculously simple ways to
teach miraculous lessons
to simple people.

Introduction

Does God ever speak to you? He speaks to me quite often. Never in an audible voice, He speaks to me through the lessons and experiences of life. This book is a compilation of many lessons that God has taught me over the years. I wrote them as editorial columns for a variety of newspapers and magazines.

The Heavenly Father has used various creative methods to teach simple truths to me, one of His stubborn children. Each chapter describes an important aspect of my relationship with our Heavenly Father, told in a way that hopefully will minister to you.

Thanks for joining me on this journey. I pray that these lessons, written as modern parables, will help you understand that Jesus really does live in our world and really wants to experience a dynamic relationship with His people. May these stories be encouraging to you, may they remind you of Christ's love, may they be lessons that help you enjoy the journey.

Because He Lives,
Trey Graham
John 3:30

Foreword

"If you like running into Jesus in the middle of ordinary circumstances, you will love *Lessons for the Journey* by new author Trey Graham. I love visiting with Trey. He makes a great traveling companion, guiding us through some interesting experiences. He sees God's hand everywhere and his passion for people flows powerfully through his journalist's pen."

–Dr. Lynn Anderson, pastor and author of numerous books, including: *If I Really Believe Why Do I Have These Doubts?*, *Navigating the Winds of Change* and *They Smell Like Sheep*.

TABLE OF CONTENTS

TABLE OF CONTENTS
(Continued)

God's Christmas Gift

In January of 1991, Andrew did what dozens of pastors and scholars only hoped to do. My friend Andrew, with no theological training or philosophical expertise, unwittingly, but unmistakably, showed me the true meaning of Christmas.

After Andrew and I returned to college from our winter break, he asked me what presents I had received for Christmas. I began to explain to him about the new clothes, the best–selling books, the popular running shoes, and all the other items on the list of precious gifts given me by family and friends. He seemed somewhat impressed, pleased at my apparent holiday windfall.

"So, Andrew, what did you get for Christmas?" I asked. Expecting to hear his wonderful list of presents, my roommate instead replied silently, holding up but one small item, an alarm clock that probably cost less than $5 at the thrift shop. "That's nice," I answered, thinking that I was sure glad that I hadn't received such a present, seemingly so small and insignificant.

Later, as roommates often do during late nights of

academic studies interspersed with stories about home, I would tease Andrew by pretending to throw that clock into the air and then catch it right before it hit the ground, feigning an attempt to damage his precious clock. Andrew never thought this game was funny, however, because his clock meant much more to him than I ever understood.

As the years passed, and our four years together at college came to a close, I noticed that while he moved from room to room and roommate to roommate, Andrew always had that same inexpensive alarm clock stored closely beside his bed. You see, Andrew's family back in West Virginia was far from wealthy, and the only present his parents could afford to give him for Christmas was that simple, unimpressive clock. What seemed like garage sale material for some families was a family treasure for Andrew.

You know what? Today, eleven years later, I cannot remember a single present I received for Christmas that year. You know what else? For the rest of my life, I will never forget Andrew's gift. While my parents bought me presents that were more elegant, more expensive, and certainly more numerous, that one single present from Andrew's parents was definitely more precious.

As this Christmas season approaches, God asked me to tell Him what was most important in my life. For what am I searching? What is my top priority? Do I value all the fancy and impressive features in life? Am I searching for notoriety and pleasure, while refusing to acknowledge what is really most meaningful in life?

Sadly, too many people will be like me this Christmas, worrying about my long list of errands, searching for that perfect present, looking for the best bargain, and miss the only gift really worth giving. Andrew's parents understood that if you can only give one gift, you had better make it special. My family and I, on the other hand, thought more was better, and more expensive meant more valuable.

God the Father has given us innumerable gifts, including life and freedom and hope and peace and health, all of which are wonderful and make life more enjoyable. One gift, however, is too important to miss. God sent His gift, His only Son, to be born as a helpless child about 2000 years ago this December. Jesus came to earth to live and to die to show me how to live, and how to die as a faithful follower of His Father, the Creator God. Yet, the parties and decorations and purchases of this commercially driven holiday season have apparently become more valuable to us than the original Gift sent to us by God.

What is important to you? Do you focus on all the

things that won't really matter in the end, or do you cherish the One who truly matters most of all? Do you even remember all the other places that you hoped to find the answers to life's questions, or were they simply more dead–ends? If my social calendar and my errands keep me from meeting Jesus this Christmas, I will truly have missed it all.

Thanks, Andrew, for helping me understand that the true meaning of Christmas is in cherishing that which matters most, the Lord Jesus Christ, rather than futilely searching after all the trappings of the world. When the advertisers encourage us to spend and buy and give, remember, "they do it to receive a perishable wreath, but we an imperishable." This Christmas, ask God for the gift of life, found only in His Son.

Character is Leaving Nothing to Chance

Character...we desperately need it and constantly search for it. My prayer for America is that we might find God, and in so doing, find God's character. What is character? Character is diligence and devotion in the little things. Character is living by the rules at all times. Character is doing what is honorable and lawful, following West Point's Cadet Prayer, which admonishes us all to "choose the harder right over the easier wrong." Character, according to H. Jackson Browne, "is what we do when we think no one is looking." Character may be the single human quality most difficult to develop and most difficult to live without.

When I arrived at Fort Wainwright, Alaska to take leadership of my first platoon at the ripe old age of 21, I met one of my more experienced soldiers, a warrant officer who had been in the army for a little over 26 years. You can imagine the tension that developed between the young leader and the veteran pilot. We eventually forged a good working relationship, and consequently, the warrant officer taught me far more about the army and about aviation than I could have ever learned in a textbook or a classroom.

Of all the lessons he taught me, however, there is one lesson I will never forget. You must remember that this man had thousands of flight hours, including several combat tours in Vietnam. This pilot knew how to fly, he knew when to fly, he knew why to fly, he apparently knew everything there was to know about flying helicopters.

Do you know what I learned? When this warrant officer, with 26 years of flying experience, got into the helicopter to take me on my first flight, he pulled out his technical manual and began to do his pre–flight checks, step by step, by the book. He prepared for this flight as if he had never flown before.

The thought entered my mind, "If anyone has an excuse to fly by memory, if anyone has the right to operate a helicopter out of habit, this man does. Yet, he follows every step in the book, as if he were flying his first mission." Then I realized that in aviation, you doing everything by the book, you leave nothing to chance. His job was too important and too dangerous to skip a step or miss an assignment. Even after 26 years of flying, he did every flight by the book, every step, every time.

In the Christian life, our character is too important to leave to chance. We cannot live holy lives by memory; we cannot glorify the Lord Jesus Christ out of habit; we cannot become godly people by accident. Our job is too important and our world needs us too much for any believer to skip a step. To be people of character, to demonstrate the character of Christ, we must live by the book, every step, every time.

If we are to be the future Christian leaders our nation desperately needs, we must become people of character. If we are going to live as God has called us to live, we must do everything by the Book, God's inspired Word. The Bible constantly reminds us that God blesses and guides the upright, while He judges harshly the ungodly. As **Proverbs 11:5** states, "The righteousness of the blameless makes a straight way for them, but the wicked are brought down by their own wickedness." America needs leaders who will guide us along the straight way, who will lead us along God's way.

In our generation, the unusual and the ungodly fascinate us. This nation has become the world's moral proving ground. Who can push the envelope of morality and decency one step further? Who can say that or show that on television? Who can perpetrate one more ungodly act, calling it freedom, or personal rights, or one's own need to express oneself? What we really need are more honest, respectable, Godly citizens. We need our young people to accept the call of God; to lead our nation to know Christ; and to make Him known. In short, our nation needs more character, not more characters.

How do we become people of character? Can I have a Godly character? Throughout history, people have sought to find and develop character, both in themselves, and in their leaders. James Froude wrote, "you cannot dream yourself into a character; you must hammer and forge yourself one." Similarly, Grenville Kleiser reminded us, "by constant self–discipline and self–control you can develop greatness of character." While character does not happen overnight, it is simply too important to overlook because it is hard to obtain, challenging to find, or so rarely demonstrated.

Character is developed through the difficulties of life. As Helen Keller explained, "character cannot be developed in ease and quiet. Only through experience of trial and suffering can the soul be strengthened, ambition inspired, and success achieved." We all say we want character, but we do not want to go through the difficulties of life. If character were easily obtained, our nation would not so desperately have to search for leaders to emulate.

Character is demonstrated in our dealings with other people. General H. Norman Schwarz-kopf said, "I admire men of character, and I judge character not by how men deal with their superiors, but mostly how they deal with their subordinates, and that, to me, is where you find out what the character of a man is." God is a God of love and, as His child, He expects me to love those people that He created in His own image, and for whom He sent His only Son to die. I demonstrate character when I treat others as God would have me, as I would hope to be treated.

Character affects how we live, both now and in the future. As Tyron Edwards explained, "Thoughts lead on to purposes; purposes go forth in action; actions form habits; habits decide character; and character fixes our destiny." Our personal and corporate destinies are going to be decided by how we live, and how we act. People of true, Godly character, love people, deal honestly with others, admit wrongs committed, accept blame when deserved, and promise to work hard to make America a better place for their having been here. One sobering truth must always remain forefront in our minds: we truly are determining our future by how we act today.

Why do we need more character in America? In this nation of religious pluralists and situational ethicists, aren't we doing just fine? The legacy of the 1990s may just be that everybody got to make his or her own rules, that no one is right or wrong, as long as we all get along. When you wonder how far our nation's morality has fallen, simply consider how far our presidency has fallen. Our nation's first president, George Washington, stated, "I hope I shall possess firmness and virtue enough to maintain what I consider the most enviable of all titles, the character of an honest man." Compare that to our later presidents, and our current standards of morality and ethics in America.

Character. Not family values, freedom of expression, personal rights, or any other media–savvy, political buzzwords. We need character, to live as God has called us to live, to return to a nation that is "holy and upright before Him." May we all remember Thomas Paine's statement, "Character is much easier kept than recovered." Sadly, America now needs to ask God to recover our national character.

If our future depended on your character, would this be the land of the free, the home of the brave, a nation of character, the greatest nation on earth? Am I a character, or do I have character? Will our next generation of leaders reject the religious plurality of the 20th Century and adopt the biblical character critically needed in the 21st Century?

Defining Christianity

Anthropologists have sought for centuries to properly define the word "peace." Every nation in the world seems to seek this state of peace, but no one is quite sure what they are looking for. Webster's New Collegiate Dictionary defines "peace" as "a state of tranquility or quiet; harmony in personal relations."

Often, however, most historians, especially military historians, choose to illustrate peace by simply defining it as the "absence of war." If you are not at war, then you must have peace. It is really a simple formula, "If you don't have 'X', you must have 'Y'."

Similarly, theologians have long tried to define the term Christianity. Dozens of different denominations and religious groups link themselves to Christ and Christianity, but obviously little consensus exists on the true form and definition of Christianity.

Without a firm conceptual idea of what Christianity is, religious people have tried to develop a concrete explanation of faith in Christ. This concrete explanation often describes the actions, or more likely, the non–actions of those who call themselves Christians.

This resulting definition often takes the form of the above definition of peace, and describes Christianity as the "absence of sin." Or, in other words, "If you don't do 'X', you must be a Christian."

Today, however, I would like to submit that the proper definition of Christianity is not "the absence of sin," but instead, the "presence of God."

While morality and righteous living ought to characterize believers in the Lord Jesus Christ, my prayer is that Christians would be known more for their actions than for their non–actions. Historically, Christians, especially my beloved Southern Baptists, have attempted to bring others to faith in Christ by laying out a formula which says, "Do 'this and that', stop doing 'thus and so', and you are ready to become a Christian."

I believe that God's Word would remind these formulaic proselytizers that morality and virtue without a true change of heart is simply rigid legalism. Does God desire for His children to live upright, moral lives? Absolutely. But our character and convictions ought to outweigh our practices and products.

God the Father did not send His Son to earth and then to Calvary in order to leave behind a cosmic list of DOs and DON'Ts. Instead, Christ came to love mankind and open the door of eternal life, allowing sinful human beings to gain access to a holy God.

If NASA trains you to push this button and read that gauge, you may appear to be a fully qualified astronaut. In reality, though, you are simply a well–trained hoax, ready for the next costume party. So, too, if your local pastor instructs you to pray this prayer, give this amount of money, and avoid this sin in order to be saved, I am afraid that Jesus will simply reply, "Depart from me, I never knew you."

Christianity, though debated and argued for two thousand years, is quite understandable and definable: simple, child–like faith, and trust in the Lord Jesus Christ. God the Father gave God the Son to pay the penalty of eternal separation caused by my sin and your sin.

People tell you to 'accomplish this', and 'avoid that'. God tells you to 'believe this', and 'receive that'. Whom would you rather trust? Whom would you rather believe?

So, what about you? What will happen when you reach the gates of heaven? Will your request for entrance include a list of sins you avoided, and good deeds you performed? Or will your guarantee of salvation include the only fact that matters, "I knew the Son of the King?"

The Truth About Friendship

Dear God,

Help me to be a friend today. Help me to be a true friend to someone who feels friendless. Allow me to love somebody who can't help me at all. Permit me to encourage one person who does not, and will not, owe me a thing. Too often, we act friendly only to those with power or prestige; I want to befriend someone who deserves friendship for who they are, not for what they have accomplished.

God, I want to make a friend today, someone who needs me and someone who needs You. It isn't always easy to make friends, though, probably because it isn't always easy to be a friend. Why do we hesitate to make friends with strangers, knowing down deep that they need friends just like we do? Funny isn't it…I make the most friends when I take that first, uneasy step and act friendly toward them, remembering Phil Callaway's statement that "no one is so empty as when he is filled with himself."

It is easy to see the solutions to problems around the world, but God, help me to see the answers to the needs of those right at home. My friends need help, Lord, and I am ready. Help me to see their needs and hurts and fears, so that I can be a true friend right when they most need the encouraging touch that only friends can bring. Lord, please help me to daily live out the principle that "He is my friend who helps me. He is more my friend who helps me to help myself. He is most my friend who helps me to help others."

I may never become famous, or I may never change the world, but I can help my friend, whomever and wherever he or she is. As Dr. Elton Mayo wrote, "One friend, one person who is truly understanding, who takes the trouble to listen to us as we consider our problems, can change our whole outlook on the world."

I can't cure their diseases, I can't heal their wounds, I can't fix their mistakes, but I can help them wait. I can sit next to them until the doctor arrives; I can hold on till their hearts stop breaking; I can wait with them until the storms of life pass.

And you know what, God? If You help me change enough friends, I really might change the world. The world is just a bunch of people like me, after all—people looking for friends.

Lord, thank you for sending the Greatest Friend, Your Son, to earth to allow me to come to You. Help me to live faithful to the One who demonstrated that "there is no greater love than this, than One who would lay down His life for His friends." Finally, God, help me to introduce my friends to the only friend that can truly meet their needs, the Lord Jesus Christ.

Oh, yea, God...thanks for being my friend first.

What Price Sin?

Dear God,

I need help, I have nowhere else to turn. I'm in too far. It hurts too much. From out there, sin looked entertaining. From up there, sin looked free. From in here, though, sin hurts. From down here, from the depths of pain and sorrow, sin controls.

Sin. Preachers preach around it, writers forget to write about it, teachers refuse to teach it—none of which excuses it—and we sit idly by as the world topples one more moral pillar in its march toward godlessness.

Sin entices, appeases, entangles, then suffocates. It grabs you, holds you, and won't let go. What looked so easy, so painless, and so free before now seems so hard, so painful, so very, very expensive.

Have we forgotten our Bibles? Lord, have we ignored your sacrifice? When we trim the Christmas tree and paint the Easter egg, do we ever stop and consider that the Jesus we flippantly celebrate died because of my sin? Is He really the reason for these seasons, or just another ornament to go with the mistletoe, chocolate eggs and candy corn?

Modern scientists search for answers to today's problems, hoping against hope to heal our pain and ease our worries. So far, though, cancer still attacks, AIDS still ravages, death still approaches. We seemingly cannot stop the onslaught of these tragic attackers, yet the ultimate malady of human history was cured two thousand years ago on a simple wooden cross between two thieves.

Imagine for a moment...God killing His own son. Really. Stop and think about that. Amazingly, mercifully, the cross provided the antidote for my disease, the balm for my pain, the security for my eternity. Wow...that is grace.

Yet, here I sit, regretting my past and reliving my guilt. That which seeks to control me, that which seeks to separate me from you, Lord, cannot, if I release myself to Jesus. Why did Jesus come? Oh yea, "To seek and to save that which is lost." Then why am I still so sinful, although I claim to serve you who are sinless?

So, God, what is the answer? What will solve the problem of sin and death? While the media has tried toleration, teachers have used education, and even the preachers have promoted inspiration, the only lasting answer to my sin problem is salvation. Holy God, help me to neglect this world and embrace your grace. Make me vigilant in my determined neglect; make me to live a life that is holy before you.

As **James 5** reminds us, "to one who knows the

right thing to do, and does not do it, to him it is sin."
Father, maybe I should have helped that person at work
who needed my aid to finish their project; maybe I should
have stopped for the guy with the flat tire; maybe I should
call that relative and say "I'm sorry." Open my eyes,
Lord, and show me what is right and what is wrong. Make
me dependent on the God of **Psalm 23**, the God who
promises to "guide me in the paths of righteousness, for
His name's sake."

Lord, never let me forget that as much as my sin
hurts me, it hurts you infinitely more. Father, also remind
me that as deep as my sin takes me, no matter how low I
feel, your loving arms are long enough to reach down and
bring me home. Thank you, God, that your sinlessness
wipes away my sinfulness, if only I will let you control
my life. Keep me near you, Lord. As the hymnwriter
sang, "Take my life and let it be consecrated, Lord, to
Thee."

Write it on my heart, Father, engrave it on my fore-
head, carve it into my tombstone: "A sinner, saved by
grace."

The Safest Place
in the World

In the summer of 1994, I visited the safest place in the United States. I can honestly say I stood in the safest, most protected room in this entire nation. During one of my visits to Washington, D.C., another Army officer, assigned to the White House Military Office, asked if I would like to experience something that few people have ever seen. I agreed, of course, and he proceeded to take me to the bomb shelter beneath the White House that would house the President and his family if nuclear attack or civil unrest ever hit the city of Washington.

This Army captain showed me the briefing rooms for the Cabinet members, the housing for the troops that would be assigned to guard our nation's leaders, and even the living quarters for the First Family. I realized at that moment that I was standing in the single most protected spot in the United States; that no other room in America could provide equal safety or protection from harm.

In my experience, then, the safest place in this country is in Washington D.C. But, the safest place in this world, the safest place in your world and mine, is wherever the sovereign God of the universe takes us. You can be no more secure, you can build no thicker walls, you can find no greater protection than being in the very center of God's divine will for your life. If God calls you to a place, you can be sure He has gone before you and prepared the way.

To a child, the loving arms of a parent provide safety and comfort that can be found in no other. For the newlyweds, a hug from a spouse says, "I will be with you always and we will make this work, together." For the Christian, when pains come and plans fail, security is found in the powerful, faithful, loving hands of the Heavenly Father.

Imagine...for Daniel, the safest place in the world was in a lion's den. For the Apostle Paul, it was in a prison; for John the Beloved, it was in exile. For Helen Keller, the safest place in the world was a silent and dark world. For Mother Theresa, she found safety in an Indian slum. For Jesus the Nazarene, the safest place in the world was on a wooden cross between two thieves.

Without God, these places would be hell. With God, these places are the classrooms that teach us character, the courtrooms where we testify of His glory, the churches in which we worship our risen Lord and Savior.

Where is the safest place in the world for you? Tim

Cypert, a youth minister in Rockwall, Texas, after recovering from a bone marrow transplant (and only receiving a 30% chance of survival), said, "I would rather have cancer and live in the will of God, than not have cancer and be out of the will of God."

Wow, that is faith. More faith than most of us will ever know. Cancer, a safe place? You bet. Why? Because God was there.

I don't know where God is going to take you. It may be Washington, D.C., it may be New York City, or it may be Abilene. God may take you to the moon, He may put you in battle, or sentence you to prison. Remember, though, wherever He sends you, He is there. And where God is, ultimate safety reigns.

As Salmon Portland Chase said in 1861, "No nation can be strong except in the strength of God, or safe except in His defense." In the White House, there are walls, and barricades, and troops, to protect the single most influential person on the planet, the President of the United States. In the safest place in the world, however, you need no walls or bombs or troops, you need only Him.

"The name of the LORD is a strong tower; the righteous run to it and are safe." **(Proverbs 18:10)** Father, take me anywhere, as long as you go with me.

There Must be More to Life Than Stuff

After spending one evening last week cleaning out a room at a home for the elderly (we call them "assisted–living quarters" in our world of political correctness), I felt obliged to ask God, "What is life anyway?" Amidst all the boxes, newspapers, walkers and wheelchairs, one entire life's worth of thoughts, experiences, hopes, dreams, and fears were contained in a 10 by 12–foot room.

It seemed so sad, so final, so cheap. Eighty–three years on this earth, eighty–three years of happiness and sadness, eighty–three years of pain and joy. Now, all that she leaves behind is eighty–three years worth of stuff. In consecutive breaths we celebrate a "long, full life" and then we start planning the garage sale.

Is this what comprises our physical life? Stuff? Whether it's worth a billion dollars, or a hundred dollars, isn't it still just stuff? Will my life, or my work, or my world, leave anything behind besides just stuff?

A man who lived a short life and never really owned much stuff asked, "What good will it be for a man if he gains the world, yet forfeits his soul?" God's Son understood that life is more than stuff, that making a good living does not always mean making a good life, and that a full house does not always correspond to a full life.

As I observed another's life come to an end, I was forced to ask questions about my own life. When that final bell rings, when my time here is over, will I have worked to earn so much as to buy so much that my legacy will be such that I made some other young soul clean out all my stuff? When people remember me, when my epitaph is read, will they say, "Man, that guy sure had a lot of good stuff?" Or, "Dear God," might they say, "Wow, that guy really did believe in his Lord. He really did love his wife."

As we cleaned out that lady's room, we packed boxes of books, and clothes, and photographs, and shoes, and lamps, and...stuff. Lots of stuff. But, beyond all the stuff, underneath all the dust, there lived a person, a person with a life. In that room, there existed a life full of memories, a life full of questions. What were the people thinking in this photo? How many family Thanksgiving dinners were eaten on these dishes? Where did they buy this? Who would have ever worn that? Where can I get one of these?

And one more question...what is life anyway? Is life made of memories, of dreams, of friendships, of acts of service and kind words? Is life prayers prayed, people helped, and hugs shared? Or, is life made up of trying to get more stuff? Must I work harder to attain that next station in life, just so I can get better stuff? After all, when the rich man dies or when the poor man dies, what do they leave behind? Stuff.

What kind of stuff do you want to leave behind? Stuff that can warm a heart, or stuff that can fill a garage? Stuff that will be shared by friends or sold by street vendors? Stuff that will brighten a day or darken a closet? Stuff that can lift people up or weigh them down?

The bumper sticker says, "He who dies with the most stuff wins." The Bible says, "He who has found his life shall lose it, and he who has lost his life for My sake shall find it." (**Matthew 10:39**)

Whom do you want to believe? Whom do you want to trust? Those who seek stuff, or He who created those who seek stuff?

God, by your grace, may what I leave behind truly lead others to follow you as they seek to make a life amidst all the stuff.

Those Who Dream Most Live Most

Dreams...the medal to be won, the road up ahead, the ideal of the young and the passion of the aged. Dreams...heavenly thoughts for earthly minds.

Some of us see dreams as the reward for our hard work and sacrifice. Most people find that their dreams are fulfilled after working and striving for many years, believing all along that tomorrow's rewards will outweigh today's sacrifices. Dreams call us to labor in the morning, and to study at night; dreams call us to pray despite being troubled and to love despite being hurt.

Carl Sandburg taught us, "Nothing happens unless first a dream." We all have personal and organizational goals we would like to accomplish, but dreams take us higher and work us harder than goals. My dream is only mine, and your dream is only yours. We all have dreams. No one in the world can keep me from dreaming...except me.

Surprisingly, the journey toward dream fulfillment may be more satisfying than the actual attainment of the dream. A sense of pride and achievement results when the team works all season to win that championship, when a student's dedication is finally rewarded at graduation. Henry David Thoreau once wrote, "I have learned this at least by my experiment: if one advances confidently in the direction of his dreams, and endeavors to live the life he has imagined, he will meet with a success unexpected in common hours."

Sometimes, however, dreams just happen. God gives us the chance to be involved in what He is doing in this world and among this people. Or maybe He gives us a special, personal desire to be something, or do something no one else could possibly ever be or do.

Dreamers need friends. Dreamers need those who will dream, hope, pray, and believe. Dreams should be shared, but only with a select few, only with those who will catch the dream and help us move toward it, believing that it can be done.

The most miserable people in the world are those without dreams—those who cannot see that finish line just around the corner; the good report coming at the next doctor's visit; the love of the friend we are just about to meet. Sadly, those who do not dream may even try to stop others from dreaming.

Today, in business, we have a lot of new phrases to help people achieve goals: "positive imagery," "company vision," and the like. Coaches say "Play like a champion today." Really, these corporate or athletic leaders are just telling you what you already know—you need to hope, you need to believe, you need to dream.

After we dream, however, we must act. Dreaming is the starting line for change, the initiation of progress, the launching pad for a new life. But, we cannot simply dream, we must act. We must start the race; we must put the soul of our dreams into the flesh and bones of reality.

My dream is to be all that God has called me to be, and to preach the Gospel of Jesus Christ to all those I meet. My dream is to love my wife and children more tomorrow than I do today. My dream is to pray more, love more, serve more, dream more. My dream is "forgetting what lies behind and reaching forward to what lies ahead, I press on toward the goal for the prize of the upward call of God in Christ Jesus" (**Philippians 3:14**)

Take a minute today and ask yourself, "What is my dream?" And then, with Stephen Leacock's reminder, "It may be that those who do most, dream most," take that step, plant that seed, say that prayer, dream that dream.

Those Who Know the Most Trust the Least

Too often, as our knowledge of God grows, our dependence upon Him decreases. Kind of depressing, isn't it? As we learn the facts about God, we tend to lose the faith in God.

How sad to think that we allow ourselves to become familiar with, used to, even bored with, the King of kings and the Lord of lords. Is it possible that we would rather explore the latest technological advances instead of the infallible Word of God? Am I more fascinated with the splendor of creation than the majesty of the Creator? Can we actually know so much about God that the supernatural becomes commonplace and the divine gets dismissed? Our generation may indeed have more knowledge about the universe, and less interest in its Maker, than any generation in human history.

The temptation to look past God is not a new one, however. Look at Simon Peter. No one spent more time on earth with Jesus than this Galilean fisherman. No one witnessed more miracles or saw more lives changed. Have we forgotten that Peter also walked on the water with Jesus? Yet Peter, the man on whom Jesus promised to build His church, denied the Christ when He needed His disciple the most. Eyewitness experience didn't necessarily bring about faithful obedience.

Abraham, called by James "the friend of God," received untold blessing and honor from God through His covenant. Unfortunately, even the father of many nations, when pressured by foreigners, denied that Sarah was his wife.

Remember that the Pharisees, who all held doctorates in the Mosaic Law, killed the Son of God enabling Him to become the Lamb of God.

Even Adam and Eve, who actually walked and talked with God Almighty, who were given nothing but the entire world to enjoy, still chose to disobey the One who had given them life.

Today, some of us feel confident to depend upon our knowledge of the intricacies of the universe for our success in this life, and also the life to come. We have decided that we need no outside help, especially from that God who, though He created us in His own image, doesn't seem to really understand the pressures and requirements of life in the 21st Century.

Why do those who know the most trust the least? Why does information preclude inspiration? Why do facts blur our faith? How can going to church hinder us from going to God in prayer?

May we all be like that woman at the well who understood no theology, who had memorized no Bible verses, who had never even been to Sunday School. All this lady knew was that she met a man named Jesus who touched her life like no one else had and asked with a child–like faith, "Is this not the Christ?" (**John 4:29**)

I wonder when in life people shift from a sense of helplessness to a sense of accomplishment, when the very blessings given us by God cause us to forget the One who gives them. I wonder when we learn to depend upon ourselves, rather than the Lord Jesus Christ, the One in Whom all things consist.

Why do those who possess the most piety demonstrate the least dedication? Why does knowing about God keep me from actually knowing God? When do I decide to trust in my strength rather than the One who gives me that strength?

Max Lucado stated this dilemma eloquently when he wrote, "The loss of mystery has led to the loss of majesty. The more we know, the less we believe. No wonder there is no wonder. We think we've figured it all out. Strange, don't you think? Knowledge of the workings shouldn't negate wonder. Knowledge should stir wonder. Who has more reason to worship than the astronomer who has seen the stars? Than the surgeon who has held a heart? Than the oceanographer who has pondered the depths?"

My prayer this year is that we will know God better than ever, and through that knowledge, learn to trust Him more than ever. New Year's often brings new commitments. Let's make a new one to Him.

Dear God, while I learn and grow, never stop showing me that though facts are important, what I really need is You.

He Must Increase

Life is full of questions. Some questions seek facts, others seek wisdom. What makes life worthwhile? How can I find fulfillment in life? Why do I feel so empty when my day–timer is so full? God, why am I so busy that I forget you? How can I, the creation, not feel obligated to bow down daily before you, the Creator?

A few nagging questions persist. What am I really doing with my life? Is my time spent doing meaningful acts, or simply spent? For whom and for what am I working? To what end am I striving? In today's society, it has become trite to ask, "What is the meaning of life?" yet so many people still don't know the answer.

I recently found a quote that expresses my desire to live a life that is worthwhile, a life that truly honors God. "One step forward in obedience is worth years of study about it."

I have spent years studying about God; I know now that He wants me to spend years obeying Him, applying all the lessons I have learned. What have you learned about God? What has He taught you? Do we really need to learn more, or do we actually need to do the things we have been taught?

Oswald Chambers wrote, "If we are in communion

with God and recognize that He is taking us into His purposes, we shall no longer try to find out what His purposes are. As we go on in the Christian life it gets simpler, because we are less inclined to say—Now why did God allow this and that? Behind the whole thing lies the compelling of God."

God has called each one of us to a specific task, namely to live obediently to His Word and His will. The exact circumstance, however, in which God places us differs from one to another. Your way is not my way; your path may not match my path. But our God is the Father of all, and we journey together, numerous individuals striving to follow different paths to the same finish line.

What is that finish line? Our earthly race is over when we enter God's heaven and hear Him say, "Well done, good and faithful servant. Enter into the joy of thy master." **(Matthew 25:21)**

My calling and your calling today are to journey toward that finish line, to serve God faithfully, to live godly lives in an increasingly ungodly world. The way may be difficult, the path may be rocky, but our mission is certain. Remember the words of Daniel Webster as you run the race, "Real goodness does not attach itself merely to this life—it points to another world."

Unfortunately, in my daily life, as I try to fulfill the call to goodness, I always seem so busy and yet never feel complete. My Bible reminds me that Jesus never rushed, yet got everything done; I am always rushed, yet never get everything done. Jesus asked His disciples, "For what will a man be profited, if he gains the whole world, and forfeits his soul?" (**Mark 8:36**)

Our society thrives on the search for a profit, but will it really make my life better, more worthwhile? Maybe that ancient philosophy shared by Jesus with a few simple fishermen does still apply today. Maybe busy–ness to profit my business is less important than my calling to be a good and faithful servant.

With a new desire to strive to honor God in all I do, I have adopted a new life verse. My life verse remains as the sure foundation when the world around me seems to crumble. This scriptural passage reminds me who really is in control. In **John 3:30**, John the Baptist declared his simple yet profound philosophy of life: "He must increase, but I must decrease." This fundamental priority for John the Baptist has become my all–consuming goal.

Life seemed overwhelming to John in the 1st Century and he needed a reminder that God still reigns. In the 21st Century, I need that same reassurance. When the stress level rises, "He must increase, but I must decrease."

When I can't seem to finish it all, "He must increase, but I must decrease." When my faith falters, "He must increase, but I must decrease." When the world seems lost and anarchy seems to reign, "He must increase, but I must decrease." When righteousness is ridiculed and evil seems victorious, "He must increase, but I must decrease."

We all should hope to live as William Law explained the Christian life in the 18th Century. "If our common life is not a common course of humility, self–denial, renunciation of the world, poverty of spirit, and heavenly affection, we do not live the lives of Christians."

So, what am I doing with my life? Is life worth living? It is more than worth it if we live for the One who gives life. As one person put it, "No one can please God without adding a great deal of happiness to his or her own life."

No matter my job title or job description, I am to faithfully obey the omniscient and omnipotent God of this universe. I set goals, I have dreams, I reach for the stars. But, after all the dust settles, when the final whistle is blown, "He must increase, but I must decrease."

Who do You Say That He is?

Each time a new officer arrives to command a military unit, for the first few weeks he will simply be referred to by his rank, such as "the captain." Although he is in charge, this man is still an outsider, one whom the troops do not know, but whose position does carry some amount of respect and authority.

Later, after a few weeks or months in command, this officer will have earned some respect and becomes known as "our captain." He has become more familiar to the troops and has begun to learn the system. When speaking about this man, the soldiers will describe the actions or decisions of "our captain" because they now know him and accept him as their commander.

One day, after the unit has accomplished an important mission and enjoyed some measure of success, once the officer has truly gained the respect and admiration of his soldiers, you will hear them refer to "my captain." Now, this commander has arrived. No longer is he an outsider they need to keep an eye on. Nor must he continue to prove himself and his commitment to the unit.

Instead, this officer has shown a love for the troops, a competency in his position, and a willingness to work with his fellow soldiers. For his commitment and his steadfastness, the commander will now be referred to as "my captain" because the troops know him, trust him, and are proud to serve under him. This officer's hard work and loyalty have paid off; he has received the greatest compliment. To the troops, he is finally "my captain."

Two thousand years ago, Jesus asked His disciples, "Who do people say that the Son of Man is?" (**Matthew 16:13**) In the next verse, the disciples then answered Jesus by saying, "Some say John the Baptist; and others, Elijah; but still others, Jeremiah, or one of the prophets."

The question today, however, is how do you refer to the Son of God, Jesus Christ? In your vocabulary, is Jesus Christ the revered Creator of the universe, or is He a curse word? When you describe Him, which possessive pronoun is affixed to His name? In your life, is Jesus the Christ, our Christ, or my Christ?

Today, Jesus Christ is asking each of us, "Who do you say is the Son of God?" In your life, is He a great leader who preached powerfully a long time ago? In your mind, is Jesus simply one of many prophets from whose teaching we ought to select profound lessons? Perhaps you have even relegated the Son of God to the status of a well–known but forgotten historical figure, alongside John Quincy Adams and Buffalo Bill Cody.

To the non–believer, to the natural man, He is "the Jesus." To the baby Christian, to the one who knows Him only vaguely, He is "our Jesus." To the mature, disciplined follower, to the one whose life revolves around Him, He is "my Jesus."

As in the first century, many people in our time consider Jesus to be a great teacher, a fine leader, a trusted prophet. While all of these qualities describe Christ, they are tragically incomplete. The disciples' answers showed that the people with whom the disciples dealt thought highly of Jesus. While these answers were flattering, they were completely wrong. Jesus is not just a faithful prophet; He is not simply a powerful religious leader or a skilled orator. Rather, Jesus Christ is the Alpha and Omega, the Prince of Peace, the Son of Man, the Lamb of God, the great I Am.

Who affects your daily life more, Jesus Christ or Peter Jennings? From whom do you seek advice, the Son of God or Dear Abby? In whose writings do you spend more time, the Apostle John or John Grisham?

I ask today, "Who do you say that He is?" Your response is as important, if not more so, than Peter's. When I ask, "Who is Jesus?" if you are only able to answer that

He is a fine man and a great prophet, I am sorry to say that you have missed the blessing of knowing and serving Him. If you cannot say, "He is my Jesus," you have missed it all.

Jesus does not need our recitation of His credentials for His sake; we need them for ours. If we see Him as Messiah and acknowledge Him as Lord, we have found eternal blessing. If we miss His lordship and admit only His good deeds, we have missed blessing and found damnation.

"Who do you say that He is?" Sounds like a simple question, but none more important has ever been asked.

If the World has Absolutes, Why Can't God?

Have you ever observed a "Right Turn Mostly" sign?

Of course not.

When the traffic safety department determines what is best for public safety, when a "Right Turn Only" sign is appropriate, no one decries their decision as exclusive or elitist. No one writes letters to their congressman demanding their freedom to turn left at this intersection.

When a person suffers a heart attack and the doctor prescribes a rigid diet, do we accuse the doctor of being rude and insensitive? Or, do we thank the physician for caring so much about the health and well being of the patient, and recommend this conscientious caregiver to our family and friends?

When the crossing guard stops children from entering a busy street in order to keep them safe from the cars, do we reprimand him for ruining the children's experience of walking to school? Of course not, we want our children to remain safe and secure, free from harm.

If a mathematics instructor gives a student a failing grade because they indicate on their exam that $2 + 2 = 5$, then we applaud the teacher for upholding the standards and teaching the student how to add properly. After all, people need to know how to add and subtract, how to pay their bills, and calculate their expenses.

Why, then, do we complain when the Creator of the universe sets a standard for our protection? Why do we rebel against the rules that God establishes? Why do we expect our Lord to grant complete freedom of choice, allowing us to determine the best way to live?

Many people in our world refuse to give their lives to Christ because they feel that a God–honoring life is too restrictive, too rigid. We expect God to let us sleep with whomever we want, whenever we want. We expect God to keep His promises to us, while we break our promises to other people. We demand that other people deal with us honestly and fairly, while we cut corners and "skim a little off the top." We recommend that people live to-gether before marriage, to "try it out," while the Bible commands that we keep the marriage bed undefiled.

I will admit to you that the Bible has absolute stan-dards that seem harsh, that seem to be inflexible accord-ing to the moral standards of the world. But, I also know three important truths about the standards that God expects His children to abide by on earth.

First, the people who say that God restricts, and therefore ruins, their lives, have never before lived the committed, Christ–like life. They are simply predicting what their reaction would be if they became faithful believers.

Second, I stand as a witness that the life that honors Jesus, with rules, restrictions, and all, is more fulfilling and more rewarding than the life that seeks only pleasure and freedom.

Third, and most importantly, God is God. You are not. Neither am I. God is the sovereign Creator and Lord, therefore He is more than qualified to direct my paths and establish guidelines for my life. After all, didn't He create this world and all the people in it?

Other fields, and other experts have rules, and they are accepted as standard practice. God has rules and we call Him a "kill–joy." Physicians establish strict dietary habits for their patients and we praise their bedside manner. God the Father prescribes strict moral habits for His people and we condemn Him as outdated and prude.

I don't understand why people, including me, rebel against spiritual authority. I only know that I am a sinner that naturally does not want to serve and obey God. Only by faith in Christ, only by the power of the Holy Spirit, only by His grace am I able to understand and obey the rules of God. We must remember God's rules are different and that He knows more and sees more than we do. The Heavenly Father instructs His children to obey His standards because "as the heavens are higher than the earth, so are My ways higher than your ways and My thoughts than your thoughts." (Isaiah 55:9)

I sure don't abide by all of God laws, but I want to. More than that, I have learned that He is the One who establishes the rules, my role is simply to obey them. Listen to your doctor, learn from your teacher, but give your life to Jesus the Savior.

What Did They Say?

Every industry and subculture has its own jargon. Every type of organization has buzzwords that help people communicate effectively and efficiently with their co–workers. These words mean something to those 'in the know', but are meaningless to those on the outside. Have you ever visited a place of business and overheard a conversation that was full of jargon? You are sure that the people are talking, but yet you have no idea what they are saying.

As a Field Artillery officer in the army, I remember numerous occasions having a conversation like this.

"Python one–six, Python one–six, Cobra Gunner."

"Python one–six, Go."

"Python one–six, Cobra Gunner, sierra papa in two zero mikes, whiskey alpha niner, niner, tree, eight, eight, one."

"Cobra Gunner, Python one–six, wilco, out."

Do you know what? That messy, confusing sentence was a complete conversation, an order from higher head-quarters telling a subordinate unit when to move. Did it make any sense to you? Probably not, unless you had been in the military and remember all the acronyms and characters in the phonetic alphabet. Yet, it makes perfect sense to people serving in the army.

People in the computer industry are notorious for using buzzwords and jargon that the average citizen does not understand. They use words like RAM, BIOS, server, byte, ASCII, gif, ISP, HTML, and DOS. These terms, used by people who program and maintain computers, don't mean much to the average person, even the average computer user, because the average person does not have the training or expertise to engage in conversations in which these terms would be used.

Did you ever try to listen to a teenager talk? Their speech is filled with what grammarians call "filler" words. These are words that are used to "fill" the silence until another, more legitimate, word is spoken. In other words, the conversations of the majority of teenage girls would be rather short without the words 'like' and 'you know'.

In addition, many interviews of professional athletes and coaches would be eliminated if you removed inconsequential phrases such as, 'we just played our game', 'they were the better team', 'we gave 110 percent', and 'we took what they gave us'. What insights do they expect us to gain from comments like that?

In the Christian church, we throw around some pretty unusual words and phrases also. In our sermons and Bible study lessons, we sometimes us words like propitiation, justification, indwelling, or salvific. As Christians, we have been known to use phrases like 'washed in the blood of the lamb', and 'slain in the Spirit'. Just what do all these phrases mean? I had to go to seminary to learn many of them, so I know that the average non–believer is lost and confused when Christians throw around church jargon.

If we want people to believe in our Savior, we have to introduce them to Jesus using their lingo, not ours. During his earthly ministry, Jesus taught using parables, short stories that dealt with topics that the average person could relate to and understand. When we teach or preach or witness, we should ensure that our vocabulary is understandable, not piously puzzling.

Bill Easum and Tom Bandy made a great impression on me recently when they stated that their ministry's goal was to answer this question. "What is it about my relationship with Jesus Christ that the world cannot live without?" The answer to that question, stated in everyday terminology and shared with people who do not know Christ as Savior, will usher in revival.

In other words, don't speak Christianese, just tell them the difference Jesus has made in your life. What attracted you to faith in Christ? How did God reach you? Share that with someone else; just share it in a manner they can understand.

As Jesus said, "Go and tell." Just go and tell in normal English.

What is Next?

It is finally over. After 36 days of lawsuits between George W. Bush and Al Gore, after dozens of press conferences in the Fall of 2000, we finally learned who would be the new President, who would lead the United States for the next four years. Now that the court fights and news flashes are over, I wonder, what did we learn from all this? Most of us received an education in constitutional law and due process during this political soap opera, but did we learn anything eternal? Can God be honored by this governmental mess?

Two men wanted to be president. Two men set as their number one priority to become Commander in Chief. You can debate the importance of the goal, you can evaluate the means taken to reach the goal, but you cannot deny either side's dogged determination to reach that goal.

My question: What is my goal? What is your goal? What consumes us? What keeps us going all day and keeps us up at night?

As a Christian, my goal must be to become more Christ–like every day. Are we as steadfast in our determination as were the presidential candidates? As William Wilberforce taught English believers two centuries ago,

"No one expects to attain to the heights of learning, or arts, or power, or wealth, or military glory without vigorous resolution, strenuous diligence, and steady perseverance. Yet we expect to be Christians without labor, study, or inquiry."

Once I set my goal, how single–minded are my efforts to reach it? Do I wake up every morning and go to sleep every evening with strategies in mind of becoming like Jesus? Do I dream about attaining that goal? Does failure to reach that goal seem like a tragedy that must be avoided at all costs?

I watched this political ping–pong match for hours on television. I witnessed these men fight to gain the nation's highest office. But I wonder, has anybody ever seen me strive to reach my goal? Everybody in America knows about the presidential fight, does anybody know that I am a Christian? Have I demonstrated my faith in Christ in a manner that is apparent to the people around me? Part of reaching one's goal is sharing it with others, seeking their help and encouragement and guidance along the way. In the church, we call that accountability.

In the presidential election and its never–ending aftermath, all decisions, all strategies were designed with one goal in mind: to become President of the United States. Everything that was done, everything these men attempted, focused on their overarching dream to be President.

We too ought to have one compelling desire that influences all our decisions: to become like Christ. May the lessons we learned during the month of debate stretch beyond constitutional idiosyncrasies and really affect our life, today and in the future. May we admire the two men for their determined desire, may we respect the winner, and may we set goals that consume us.

Can America really be better off after this struggle than before? It can, and will, if you and I, folks who will probably never become president, emulate the goal setting and goal chasing of our candidates. Let us resolve to be better people and better Christians as we set high goals and work tirelessly to achieve them.

Lessons Learned on the Mission Field

Recently, I returned home after spending nine days in Guatemala as part of a missions project with my church. Seventeen members of our church had the privilege of working with Deidrea Johnson of Helps International, an organization that seeks to meet the physical and spiritual needs of the people of this Central American nation.

While I was on the trip to Guatemala, I received an e–mail from a friend of mine. He asked, "How was the trip? What did you do? What did you learn?" His questions led me to think through the many lessons that God revealed to me while on this mission trip. This list was my response to his question, but more so, this was my way of sorting through my thoughts and thanking God for teaching me each of these important, yet all too often forgotten, lessons.I learned that we have way too much stuff, and that stuff does not make people happy.

❑ I learned that simplicity in life is a good thing.

- ❏ I learned that we are all God's children, created in His image, no matter where we live or what language we speak.

- ❏ I learned that teams who are unified can do amazing projects, more than they ever would have imagined, if they will commit themselves to a higher task and work together in unselfish unity.

- ❏ I learned that all people need friendship, smiles, sharing, teamwork, direction, and encouragement.

- ❏ I learned that God calls us to a much higher work than we have ever experienced or participated in before.

- ❏ I learned that Christ's love is universal, and we should try every day to replicate that love in our own lives.

- ❏ I learned that serving the needs of others is more satisfying that serving one's own desires.

- ❏ I learned that Christ died for all mankind, and that our highest calling on earth is to share that truth with all people, regardless of their reaction.

- ❏ I learned that I really don't work hard enough, relax enough, greet strangers enough, get up early enough, or help my neighbors enough.

- ❏ I learned that everyone has a role to play, and a contribution to make, in order to successfully complete the mission.

- ❏ I learned that saying you love someone is not enough.

- ❏ I learned that it is a rare treat to reunite with old friends.

- ❏ I learned that new friends who are willing to serve along my side are just waiting for me to reach out to them.

- ❏ I learned that I value, love, and miss my wife and children more when I am away than when I am with them.

- ❏ I learned that how much money you have in the bank matters almost none at all, but how much of God's love you have in your heart matters most of all.

- ❏ I learned that life without microwaves, televisions, cellular phones, radios, cars, hot showers, and air conditioning is really not that bad.

- ❏ I learned that bigger houses don't equal happier families.

- ❏ I learned that true joy comes from serving Christ by serving His people.

For some of you, these lessons are new and radical. They don't seem to match up to the standards of today's society. For some of you, these lessons may seem like a blast from the past. You were taught truths like these by your godly parents many years ago. For me, these are lessons that I hope will stay with me. God opened my eyes to His work in His world, and I hope He will allow me to participate again in some small way. May we all be on mission for Christ, obeying the Great Commission, and embodying the Great Commandment.

I'm With Him

When I was stationed in Alexandria, Virginia, I had the opportunity to visit many of our nation's most sacred historical landmarks. During one of my visits to Washington, D.C., I received a tour of the White House office complex. My escort, a Captain, showed me around the various offices and agencies that work in the White House and pointed out the beautiful photographs that hang on the walls throughout the building. These pictures show the President and his family on their official state visits, as well as during personal trips and private moments as they travel around the country. There are also photographs of other members of the American government in famous places throughout the world.

The Captain explained to me that these photos are displayed in the hallways of the White House for several weeks and then are replaced by newer shots. Once the pictures are taken down, some are saved and stored in the White House archives, but most are given away to people who work in the building. The photos are given to the highest–ranking person who has happened to reserve that particular shot by writing his or her name on the back of the frame.

My escort stated that on many occasions, he would

have loved to been the recipient of some of these photos, many of which depict significant events in American history. Knowing that a captain will rarely outrank anyone at the White House, however, he realized that he had little chance of receiving the photo gifts. Therefore, he used someone else's name in place of his own.

You see, the Captain worked for a Colonel in the White House Military Office, and to get pictures, he put the Colonel's name on the back of the photos. The Captain understood that the Colonel, due to his higher rank, had a much better chance of receiving the pictures, so he put the Colonel's name on the back hoping that the Colonel would agree to give these photographs to the Captain and his family. In other words, this Captain claimed the authority of someone higher ranking in order to accomplish one of his goals.

In the same way, unbelievers have no spiritual authority in God's heavenly kingdom, but Christians have the distinct privilege of claiming the authority of our Savior, Jesus Christ. The name of Jesus Christ empowers His followers when we face trials and difficulties in this life because we are "joint heirs with Him," as promised in **Romans 8:16–17**. This passage explains to each of us that if we have come to a saving knowledge of Jesus Christ, then we are "joint heirs" with Christ to the riches of the throne of the Almighty God.

Before I came to know Jesus Christ as my Savior, I was a sinful outsider who intruded into the presence of a holy God; I was someone who possessed no rank or authority. Today, as a born–again believer, I am now a family member who is known, loved, and welcomed by Almighty God into the holy of holies.

Therefore, as Christians, we do not live in our own earthly power, but live by the power of God that lives within us once we accept Jesus Christ as our Lord and Savior. This Heavenly power allows us to resist the temptations of the world because Jesus lived a sinless life as our example. While on earth, Jesus had "been tempted in all things as we are, yet without sin" (**Hebrews 4:15**).

Therefore, Jesus understands the difficulties and hardships we face in life. Our prayer times allow us to bring our needs and concerns to a loving Father, not some oblivious celestial being. God the Father loves us and saves us through the sacrifice of God the Son. In order to be successful in the Christian life, we must adopt the power of Christ and admit our personal spiritual power-lessness. As the Apostle Paul explained to the Corinthian church, "we walk by faith, not by sight" (**II Corinthians 5:7**).

Just as my escort in the White House realized that the only way he would be able to receive the White House photographs was by connecting himself to the authority of the Colonel, Christians must understand that the only way to live this life victoriously, and the only way to ensure eternity in God's presence, is to commit ourselves to the Lord Jesus Christ as Savior.

What Are We to be?

What has God called the Church of Jesus Christ to be? Theologians throughout history have suggested various metaphors to explain what the Church is, and to illustrate its function. What is our mission? Who is our assigned target?

I submit that, as the Church, we need to be a MASH, not a VFW. A MASH is a place where hurt people go to be healed. A VFW is a place where retired soldiers go to talk about battles they fought decades ago.

According to the U.S. Army, "the primary function of a Mobile Army Surgical Hospital (MASH) is to do emergency, life–saving surgery and to make the patient transportable to rear medical installations." In a MASH, doctors and nurses constantly look for the next hurting person, diagnose their need, and apply the proper measures to see healing take place.

In the MASH of Christianity, we ought to desperately search for the next spiritually wounded soul and apply the only medicine that works, the Gospel of Jesus Christ. In **Psalm 147:3**, we read about the spiritual medicine that Christ brings; "He heals the brokenhearted and binds up their wounds." As the Church, our responsibility is to bring hurting people to the Great Physician. We heal no wounds, He heals all wounds, so we must be willing to face the dangers of battle in order to find and bring people to Christ.

In a VFW, the organization for Veterans of Foreign Wars, old men and women talk about the battles they experienced together many years ago, but fail to point out that they have not seen combat in years. Our country ought to honor and thank the soldiers who fought valiantly in battle many years ago; our churches should not. Christian soldiers who have not been to battle in years need retraining, not recognition.

Our nation needs VFW chapters; our churches do not. Instead of celebrating past battles, our churches need to locate and occupy the front line in today's spiritual battles. Spiritual warriors are prepared to fight for their cause today, not talk nostalgically about yesterday's battle.

The VFW national headquarters stated their four cornerstones of the VFW organization. These goals support an excellent veterans' organization, but they do not reflect the missionary fervor of the Church of Jesus Christ.

First, the VFW works to preserve veterans' rights. America should preserve veterans' rights, for these men and women risked their lives to defend democracy. As Christians, we have no rights except to take up our cross daily and follow Him.

Second, the VFW advocates a strong national defense. Our nation needs a strong defense, ready to protect our families and our homeland against all enemies. The Church of Jesus Christ needs to be on the offense, not waiting for attacks, but aggressively spreading the Good News.

Third, the VFW promotes patriotism in the United States. Patriots love their country and devote themselves to its preservation. America is a great nation and we ought to thank the Father for blessing this land. Faithful believers need to love their Savior more than their nation, be more concerned about lost souls than election results or legislative agendas.

Finally, the Veterans of Foreign Wars hopes to offer their assistance in community service projects. As Christians, we ought to be more committed to community service than many of the secular organizations are. Hundreds, even thousands, of secular organizations exist for the purpose of healing the broken and downcast. Why don't our churches take the lead and minister earthly peace and eternal security to the "least of these my brethren?" (**Matthew 25:45**)

Most churches fail to live up to this standard of commitment to community service. May we be reminded that Jesus said, "Your love for one another will prove to the world that you are my disciples." (**John 13:35**) If I love Christ, I am His disciple. If I am His disciple, I am to love others. If I love others, I am to share with them the good news of salvation, even if that sharing requires encountering the dangers of combat.

As a MASH, we must stand guard on the front lines of battle, ready to locate the spiritually wounded and give medical treatment when needed. In **John 3:17**, we read, "For God did not send his Son into the world to condemn the world, but to save the world through him." The Gospel is our medicine, the antidote for the disease of sin. Let's not sit and talk about the victories of the past, let's fight the battles of today.

MASH doctors treat wounded soldiers and apply all necessary measures to see them healed and returned to combat duty. As Christians, we must apply all necessary measures to see people healed spiritually and equipped to combat the enemy for the cause of Christ. We need to train our doctors, the believers in our local churches, to have the medical training necessary to share the healing power of the Gospel with lost friends and neighbors.

The battle is long and the casualties are mounting. Our world desperately needs a Savior, and, therefore, it desperately needs the Church of Jesus Christ to stand its post. We must provide the curative treatment that a MASH is designed to give, and boldly speak the Good News of healing to the hurting. Military soldiers who bravely fought the enemy deserve a break; Christian soldiers need to stop fearing the enemy and get in the fight. We must remember the promise in **I John 4:4**. "You are from God, little children, and have overcome them; because greater is He who is in you than he who is in the world."

Submit to God's Authority

In the army, officers have authority because of their rank and their job title. Most of the time, soldiers respond well to rank and obey the orders given them. Sometimes, however, their compliance is preceded by questions of: "Why?" "How?" and "Are you sure?"

During my time as a platoon leader, I changed platoon sergeants as one soldier rotated from the unit and a new one arrived in replacement. After the new platoon sergeant arrived, he took over this important role as the senior non–commissioned officer in the platoon. Shortly after his arrival, we deployed for our first military exercise together and I gave him his first order.

Expecting the need to explain myself further, I was caught off guard by his response. My new platoon sergeant, after receiving his mission, said simply, "Yes, Sir." That was it. No request for additional information, no desire to debate, just a simple "Yes, Sir."

I was taken aback by this soldier's acceptance of

my authority. After having dealt so long with troops who wanted to know why and when and how, it was refreshing to meet someone who wanted to do their job simply because the boss said so. This sergeant correctly understood that he worked for me, that I had developed the plan, and he was to execute that plan. His respect and loyalty were refreshing.

Then, as He usually does, God asked me a question. "Do you respond to me as quickly and respectfully as you want those soldiers to respond to you?"

As believers, how often do we say, "Yes, Sir" to God, salute smartly, and move on to accomplish the missions given us? Or, how often do we try to debate the Creator of the universe on the merits of His divine will? How frequently do we seek to suggest new possibilities to the Father, just in case He has not thought everything through?

Who among us has the right to question God's decisions? Who among us knows more than the omniscient Lord of Glory?

I have come to understand that my new platoon sergeant responded properly and positively to my orders, not because he was inexperienced or immature, but because he had been in the army for many years and understood the military rank structure. Whereas many of my younger and less experienced soldiers felt the need to question my decisions and offer their suggestions, this experienced NCO understood that the platoon leader was in charge, even if you disagreed with his decisions.

In the Christian Army, we need mature believers who willingly and immediately respond to God's call, without debate or doubt. Many of our members who have not yet grown to the highest levels of spiritual maturity feel that God's plan is open for discussion, that His divine will needs our input.

As a platoon leader, I did not need the advice of a private. As the King of kings and Lord of lords, God does not need my recommendations. He simply wants my devotion. As a seminary professor once told me, "In the Christian life, there is no success or failure. There is only obedience."

The Apostle Paul wrote that the job of Christian soldiers is to "be strong in the Lord, and in the strength of His might." (Ephesians 6:10) God has a plan, God is the victor. He needs not my guidance, but I desperately need His.

To grow spiritually, we need to listen to God more and question Him less. To win spiritual battles, we need to obey our commander, we need to recognize His authority, we need to salute our King and follower wherever He leads. Don't ask for His explanation; instead, ask for His guidance and for His strength. Then, like my platoon sergeant, just follow.

The Basics of Scripture

In God's Word, the Lord gives us a few basics truths that are fundamental to our spiritual growth as Christians. I admit that there are a few passages in the Bible which are so deep and theological that they are hard for many to understand. However, our Heavenly Father has also given us many truths that are so basic, so comprehensible, that any person can understand and implement in their own lives.

We need to study these fundamental truths, because our problem is not one of understanding, it is one of obedience. As has been well said, "The purpose of Bible study is application, not interpretation." I honestly believe that if we would spend more time studying and implementing these basic truths, the level of our Christ–likeness would increase exponentially. Also, once I begin to demonstrate the basics of the Christian life, my mind is more open and more ready to understand the deeper truths of the faith.

So, what are some of these basics? What must I do to grow in Christ? How can I know God better today?

Before we start another debate about theological intricacies, let's commit ourselves to applying these few verses
from the New Living Translation.

❑ *If you are not sure where we all came from...*
"In the beginning God created the heavens and the
earth." **Genesis 1:1**

❑ *If you are not convinced that God really loves you...*
"For God so loved the world that he gave his only
Son, so that everyone who believes in him will not
perish but have eternal life. God did not send his
Son into the world to condemn it, but to save it."
John 3:16–17

❑ *If you want to know how to live this life...*
"So, you see, it is impossible to please God without
faith. Anyone who wants to come to him must believe that there is a God and that he rewards those
who sincerely seek him." **Hebrews 11:6**

❑ *If you want to know how to deal with other people...*
"Your love for one another will prove to the world
that you are my disciples." **John 13:35**

❑   *If you want to know what your first priority ought to be...*
"You must worship no other gods, but only the Lord, for he is a God who is passionate about his relationship with you." **Exodus 34:14**

❑   *If you want to know the key to salvation...*
"For if you confess with your mouth that Jesus is Lord and believe in your heart that God raised him from the dead, you will be saved. For it is by believing in your heart that you are made right with God, and it is by confessing with your mouth that you are saved." **Romans 10:9–10**

❑   *If you want to know if you really need a Savior...*
"For all have sinned; all fall short of God's glorious standard." **Romans 3:23**

❑   *If you ever wondered how to get a ticket to heaven...*
"For the wages of sin is death, but the free gift of God is eternal life through Christ Jesus our Lord." **Romans 6:23**

❑   *If you ever wondered who really was in charge...*
"The earth is the Lord's, and everything in it. The world and all its people belong to him." **Psalm 24:1**

❑   *If you have ever been unsure of what to do next...*
"If you need wisdom—if you want to know what God wants you to do—ask him, and he will gladly tell you. He will not resent your asking." **James 1:5**

Isn't God's Word amazing? So simple that a child can understand it, yet so complex that all the scholars in the world have not yet fully explained everything contained therein.

There is a time for complex, in–depth Bible study. But, today, just for today, let's forgo the dissection of historical settings and the parsing of Greek verbs. Let's just commit ourselves to studying, doing, even memorizing these ten passages.

Ten passages that can change our lives; ten passages that can change our world. Tomorrow, let's go back to pondering esoteric nuances—today, let's just read and do what God says.

Why Pick Second Best When First Place is Waiting?

Have you ever read about the gymnast who, after earning a gold medal, chose to accept the silver instead? Have you ever witnessed someone stating his or her preference to be named salutatorian instead of valedictorian? In your experience, do you know anyone who declined a raise because they felt the company owed that money to another, more deserving employee?

Have you ever experienced any of these? Of course not. Why? Because we know that first is best, that primary is better than secondary, that no one would ever choose second best when first place is waiting.

In **John 9:29**, the Pharisees, a group of influential Jews in Palestine who were known for their accurate interpretations and zealous observance of Jewish law, announced, "We know that God has spoken to Moses; but as for this man, we do not know where He is from." They expressed their doubts about the spiritual authority of

Jesus of Nazareth. These Jewish scholars, numbered by Josephus to be about six thousand strong in Jesus' day, were confident in the godliness and character of Moses, but were unsure about the religious qualifications of an itinerant preacher who happened to be the son of Joseph and Mary.

Earlier in the Gospel of John, the author writes, "For the Law was given through Moses; grace and truth were realized through Jesus Christ." (**John 1:17**) In other words, God's judgment and wrath were given through Moses, as seen in the law; God's grace and love were given through Jesus, demonstrated by the cross. Yet, in the first century, some people still preferred to believe in Moses rather than Jesus. For centuries, and even today, some Jews prefer to place their faith in Moses, God's chosen leader, rather than in Jesus Christ, God's only begotten Son.

In your life, have you ever picked the difficult road over the smooth road? Have you ever chosen the painful way over the painless way? Would you prefer judgment if grace were available? The Pharisees did, because they believed that their pious living was holy enough to allow them to escape the judgment. Thus, they felt that they did not need God's grace.

Sadly, when their lives ended, they learned in death

what we must all learn in life. Your pious deeds and my good works are not enough to allow us to escape judgment. In faith, "all our righteous deeds are like a filthy garment." **(Isaiah 64:6)**

As sinful human beings, we cannot escape judgment, we can only beg for mercy. The Pharisees were too proud to admit their need for a Savior. Thankfully, by God's grace, I am too sinful to be deluded by my own righteousness. I know I need a Savior. I know you need a Savior. His name is not Moses.

Moses was a godly man, a talented leader, a skillful administrator, a trusted deliverer. Yet, Moses was also a murderer and a coward. Moses knew he was not the Savior, but the Pharisees, who knew the law but not the God of the law, failed to understand that.

Who was Jesus of Nazareth? In John chapter 18, Pilate asked Jesus if He were a king. Jesus answered, "You say correctly that I am a king. For this I have been born, and for this I have come into the world, to bear witness to the truth. Everyone who is of the truth hears My voice." **(18:37)**

What is the truth? How can you know the truth? Jesus Himself explained in **John 14:6**, "I am the way, and the truth, and the life; no one comes to the Father, but through Me."

In this verse, Jesus explains the exclusive plan of salvation. He gives the solitary roadmap to heaven. You do not receive eternal life by believing in Moses, but by placing your faith and trust in Truth Himself, the Lord Jesus Christ. Salvation comes not by Moses, Abraham, Elijah, John the Baptist, John Wesley, Billy Graham, or Martin Luther King, Jr. Everlasting salvation comes only by the Savior of all these men, God's promised Messiah, a carpenter born in Bethlehem named Jesus Christ.

Why pick second best when first place is waiting to receive you? Why pick Moses when Jesus is calling out to you? Why pick a human when you could pick God Himself? Why depend on your strength when the Creator of the universe offers you His power?

Don't pick Moses; pick Moses' Messiah. You need a Savior; I need a Savior. We all need to know God and we can only know Him through His Son. Give the control of your life to Jesus, ask Him to be your Savior. Don't pick second best when first place is waiting.

Natural Drift

No one likes getting lost. It has become a cliché to joke about men refusing to ask for directions. No one enjoys the feeling of not knowing where they are or where they are headed.

In the army, soldiers find their way through the woods or the desert by using a technique called Land Navigation. "Land Nav" allows a soldier to move through the woods on foot without getting lost. With this method, the soldier, using his compass and a map, picks a point in the distance that he knows is along the right path, called an "azimuth," and then walks the short distance to that point. He then picks another point along the correct path and walks to it. The soldier repeats this process until he finally reaches his intended destination.

Of the many potential pitfalls of using the Land Navigation method, the most dangerous is the effect called Natural Drift. Natural drift occurs when a soldier unknowingly wanders off course. The usual cause of this drift is the pull of gravity. When you are walking along the side of a hill that slopes downhill to your right, you will gradually drift off your course to the right because the force of gravity will pull you off the straight path a little at a time. Finally, over time, you have drifted a great distance off the correct path and you are nowhere near your intended destination.

Natural drift is obviously a problem because your ability to accomplish the mission is damaged or eliminated if you are in the wrong location. Natural drift is especially dangerous, however, because you don't even notice that it is occurring. In other words, the soldier who gets off course is getting "loster and loster" without ever knowing it, drifting further and further off course as the effect of gravity continues to pull him downhill.

When doing land navigation in the woods, if I take my eyes off the known target in the distance, I will drift along the natural slope of the hill. In the Christian life, if I take my eyes off God, I will begin to fall into the natural habits and actions of the world. The world seeks to pull me away from Christ, but seldom are the world's techniques of influence overt. Instead, the enemy uses the temptations of the flesh to divert our attention from our intended destination, serving Christ faithfully, and we begin to drift.

I know that I don't have to tell you that living a faithful Christian life seems unnatural, that we seem to need a miraculous dose of the Spirit's power each day just to stay the course. Yet, God did not design it that way. God the Father created us to know Him and serve Him, to enjoy doing it, and "to keep ourselves unstained by the world" (**James 1:27**). As Jurgen Moltmann wrote in The Way of Jesus Christ, "Jesus' healings are not supernatural miracles in a natural world. They are the only natural things in a world that is unnatural, demonised and wounded."

Our sinful, lost world is indeed spiritually unnatural and the only truly "natural' life is one that is plugged into the supernatural, the Creator God, our Heavenly Father. We are not to "be conformed to this world" (**Romans 12:2**), but set aside according to the laws of God. God has called us to be separate and holy, not overcome by the temptations that we face in this life.

As we drift away from Christ and toward the world, we begin to look less and less like God and more and more like an ungodly world. Bill Hybels described one instance of natural drift when he wrote that "the archenemy of spiritual authenticity is busyness, which is closely tied to something the Bible calls *worldliness*—getting caught up with this society's agenda, objectives and activities to the neglect of walking with God."

As Christians, if we continually walk with the world, we will begin to drift off course. Our focus must remain on Christ, and it must remain sharp, not blurred by the busyness or temptations we all face. A. J. Gossip wrote in The Galilean Accent, "You and I drift on through the years dully enough, because we do not believe in God, not really, and so we have no expectation. But Jesus did believe in Him, was sure He is alive and abroad in the world; that, therefore, anything may happen any hour."

Natural drift is quiet yet deadly. What is simply a small deviation at first becomes a huge gap between where you are and where God intended you to be. We must keep our eyes on the true target, the Lord Jesus Christ, in order to stay on the straight and narrow path that leads to life. Keep on your path, focused on Christ, and refuse the world's attempts to pull you off course. Don't drift toward the natural, stay connected to the supernatural.

With A New Life Comes A New Name

Python one–six. That was my name in the army, my call sign. During military exercises or deployments, no one called me Trey, or even Lieutenant Graham, only Python one–six. The army gave me a new name based on my job, my duties and responsibilities.

I was the platoon leader for the Python platoon, so my call sign was Python one–six, my commander was Cobra six, and our battalion commander was Dragon six. Everyone in the army has a job to do and that job is assigned a call sign, a new identity, a new name.

What is your name? Maybe its Bob, or Mary, or David, or Sue. What does the world call you? Does your position in life give you a new name? Some of you are called Coach, Teacher, Doctor, or Reverend. Like the army, maybe the world refers to you by your job title. Some of you may be important, and therefore the world calls you Boss, Sir, Ma'am, Mister, or Miss.

But, maybe the world isn't quite so kind to you. Maybe the world calls you dumb, or dirty, or unimportant, or maybe even unnecessary. The world, and especially some of the people we see most often, refer to us based on the way they see us, what they want us to be, what we should be in their eyes. Often, if we do not measure up to someone else's standards, they give us ugly, hurtful names.

God also calls you names based on how He sees you. He calls you His child, His adopted one, the joint heir with Christ Jesus the King. He calls you blessed, redeemed, saved, anointed. God gives you these names after you come to know His Son, the Savior Jesus Christ.

While the world may call you unpleasant and insensitive names, God gives you names that heal and love. Jesus renamed His disciple known as Simon. Jesus gave Simon the name Petros. In English, we call him Peter. Simon got this new name because he had a job to do, just like I got the name Python one–six from the army because I had a job to do. Peter's job was to be the foundation of the Church of Jesus Christ. Simon's new name, Peter, means "rock" and Jesus promised to build His church upon this rock.

God gives us new names and He gives us jobs to do in His kingdom. When I know God through His Son

Jesus, He assigns me a mission and gives me new names that remind me that He loves me and will help me faithfully accomplish my assignments. I received a new identity when I joined the army, and I received a new identity when I joined God's army and became His child.

What does the world call you? The world's name for you may encourage you or hurt you, but in the end, it doesn't really matter. What does God call you? That makes all the difference in the world. If He calls you son, or daughter, you can be sure you will spend eternity with Him in a real and glorious place called heaven. If He calls you stranger, may I now introduce you to the One who gives us new names and new life, the Savior, Christ Jesus the Lord?

The Key to the Kingdom

During the summer of 1992, I was assigned to work at the Army Research Institute in Alexandria, Virginia. One day during my tour of duty there, I attended the retirement ceremony of a four–star general and the assumption of command ceremony for his successor, another four–star general.

When I walked in the door, the master sergeant who was serving as the hostess for this event assumed that I was the son of one of the two generals who were being honored that day, so she quickly escorted me down to the front row of the auditorium. Since she believed I was the son of the general, she politely asked an Israeli colonel to please leave his seat so that I could have it. I immediately declined this offer and told the colonel to keep his seat, and then I headed to my rightful spot, standing in a corner in the back of the room.

Although I was the lowest ranking officer in the room, and therefore held no authority whatsoever, the master sergeant assumed I was the son of the commanding general and therefore must be important. While I felt intimidated and scared, she thought I possessed great rank and power. I had no business sitting down front during this retirement ceremony, but because I supposedly knew the boss, I could sit wherever I wanted.

In the Christian life, as believers, we have bold access into the throne room of God the Father simply because we know His Son.

The master sergeant in Washington, D.C. assumed I was a son and enjoyed full access and intimacy with a general who outranked me, knew far more about the army than I will ever know, and has seen more in his military career than I will ever see. I, however, viewed myself as an outsider who was merely visiting, almost intruding upon, this general's finest hour, his retirement ceremony.

Before I came to know Jesus Christ as my Savior, I was a sinful outsider who intruded into the presence of a holy God, someone who possessed no rank or authority. Today, as a born–again believer, I am now a family member who is known, loved, and welcomed by Almighty God into the holy of holies.

Why does He invite me in? Because I have accomplished great things or helped numerous people? No. Maybe because I try very hard to live the right kind of life? Wrong again. God allows me into His heaven for one reason, because I know His Son, and in fact, am a son of God myself because I have been saved by the grace of God through faith in Jesus Christ.

Do you feel like you intrude upon God when you try to pray? Do you feel like you possess no spiritual authority? Do you want access to the God of the universe? Simply ask His Son to show you the way. Pray to Jesus that He would save you and introduce you to His Father.

The Gift of Life

When I was a senior in high school, I received a scholarship from a college that I had no intention of attending. While I appreciated their offer, I did not want to attend this school in this state, so I declined. Then I realized that I had a friend who attended that college and he sure could use some scholarship money.

So, in an act that made perfect sense to a seventeen year old, I called this school (collect, by the way) and asked if I could share my scholarship with my friend, Joe. While I was grateful for their generous offer, I knew someone who could really use that scholarship money and he was already a student at their fine institution.

Well, the registrar's office enthusiastically explained to me that I had neither the right nor the authority to volunteer my scholarship to another student. This scholarship offer was made directly from the school to me, a free gift that was not intended to be used by any other students.

I tried to explain to them that I had my own scholarship money and my friend really needed financial help, so it would seem pretty logical that I pass along this scholarship offer to Joe. Unfortunately, they explained, the rules of college financial aid prevented the arrangement I was suggesting. The money was designed only for me and could not be transferred to another person.

As I studied God's Word recently, He reminded me that His gift of grace cannot be transferred from person to person either. God's free offer of salvation comes directly from God Himself to a specific person, just like that scholarship offer came directly from the school to me. While I could not share the scholarship money with Joe, neither can I share my salvation with others, no matter how badly they need it, or how desperately I want them to accept it.

Salvation is found only in the Lord Jesus Christ, by believing that His death on the cross of Calvary, and the resurrection celebrated at Easter, guarantee eternal life. We all have relatives and friends that we wish would believe in Christ and accept His offer of salvation. Sometimes, we want them to come to Jesus so badly we are even willing to repent and believe for them. Unfortunately, while Christianity is best celebrated corporately, it is only accepted individually.

As a minister, I am often asked, "How do you go to heaven?" Or, "What is salvation?" Some even say, "Can you really know God while you are on earth?" Let's review the scriptures for a minute and try to answer these questions. In **John 14:6**, Jesus stated, "I am the way, and the truth, and the life; no one comes to the Father, but through Me."

This verse explains two important truths. First, Jesus offers to share with us the way to truth and eternal life. Second, while there are many roads to spirituality, there is only one route to heaven, through faith in the Lord Jesus Christ.

In **II Corinthians 5:17**, the Apostle Paul writes, "Therefore, if any man is in Christ, he is a new creature; the old things have passed away; behold, new things have come." If I seek to find the way to heaven that Jesus offers, I will not only find eternal life in heaven, I also receive a new life here on earth. My old life, my old sins, my old pains pass away and are replaced by new life, new goals, new reasons to live.

How does one find this new life? How does one become a new creature? Paul also wrote in **Romans 10:9–10**, "if you confess with your mouth Jesus as Lord, and believe in your heart that God raised Him from the dead, you shall be saved; for with the heart man believes, resulting in righteousness, and with the mouth he confesses, resulting in salvation."

While it seemed like a good idea for me to share my scholarship money with Joe, the rules established by the college would not allow it. They did not dislike Joe, but you have to receive your own scholarships by following the rules of the school, not by borrowing from others. While many religions offer purpose in life on earth or salvation through life in heaven, one has to find God according to His rules. I cannot accept Jesus Christ as Savior for you, and you cannot open the doorway to heaven for me.

Are you still searching for meaning in life? Have you found the way to earn your place in heaven yet? Why don't you follow the plan of God and accept Christ as your Savior, placing your trust in the One who said, "Come to Me, all who are weary and heavy–laden, and I will give you rest?" Do you need rest? Do you need purpose in life? You need Christ, the greatest Christmas gift of all.

Unknown Soldiers: Anonymous, Yet faithful

As Americans, we honor and revere the Unknown Soldiers, those men who anonymously gave their lives to serve and defend our nation. In Arlington National Cemetery lie the three soldiers who have received the highest military honors, including the Congressional Medal of Honor, while no one even knows their names. As the plaque reads, this tomb is "Where Valor Proudly Sleeps." The soldiers who guard this tomb memorize the Sentinels' Creed, which says in part, "It is he who commands the respect I protect. His bravery that made us so proud. Surrounded by well meaning crowds by day alone in the thoughtful peace of night, this soldier will in honored glory rest under my eternal vigilance."

In God's army, the greatest works of revival and evangelism occur due to the efforts of unknown Christian soldiers. The Christian Church needs more soldiers who are willing to work, to serve, to die in order to see the mission accomplished. The finest, most trustworthy sol-

diers are those who work not for medals, awards, or recognition, but instead to protect one's brothers and finish
one's missions.

While a few soldiers receive acclaim and honor for
their heroic deeds, the great majority of soldiers defend
their country quietly, anonymously, simply because it is
their job, their duty. As Christian believers, we need more
faithful, humble soldiers who serve not for awards and
recognition, but simply to do their duty to serve Christ
and to bring others to Him.

You know the names of a few famous soldiers who
have demonstrated bravery and honor during times of
harrowing danger. But, you know not the untold millions
of American men and women who have served this nation
faithfully, quietly, heroically. In the Church of Jesus
Christ, we have a few famous, recognizable leaders. But, I
believe God would have us to know the untold millions
who throughout the centuries have served in the Army of
God faithfully, quietly, heroically.

Are you a soldier for God? Have you enlisted in His
army by taking the oath of allegiance called the prayer of
salvation? If you have not, may I invite you to join the
only army guaranteed to win every battle, every time? If
you are already a soldier of Christ, are you seeking to
advance the cause of your commander, or do you seek

medals and public notoriety?

May we all seek to be soldiers of God, unknown soldiers of Christ, who faithfully serve God because our duty is to glorify Him, not to make a name for ourselves. God bless the Unknown Soldiers of Christ.

Why Do We Serve God Anyway?

Growing up, I really hated to work in my grandmother's yard. Several times a month, I would travel the few miles to her house and help her pull weeds, plant green beans and tomatos, mow the grass, trim the bushes, among other various chores. I "volunteered" for this duty because my grandmother asked me to help her. You must know, however, that I really went because my father made me.

Can I share something with you? I don't like green beans. Yet, there I was, planting green beans, adding fertilizer, pulling weeds, all for vegetables that I would never eat. Not only do I not like green beans, I am not crazy about gardening. My non–green thumb views yard work as a necessary evil at best, a burdensome chore at worst. Obviously, I was never thrilled about the chance to work in my grandmother's garden. While I loved her, I could live without her yard.

Later, during my senior year of high school, my grandmother went to be with the Lord, dying in her sleep. So, at the age of 18, I was left with only one grandparent still alive. After her death, I often thought about Maw-

Maw and looked back on those hot days working in the garden, pulling weeds and mowing grass. I remembered the hard work, but I also fondly remembered the special, quality times she and I had shared while I was helping her keep up her house and yard.

A few years later, while I was in college, someone asked me if there was anything in my life that I would change if I had the chance. I thought for a few moments and realized that they expected for me to say that I would have attended a different university or have been more successful in my athletic career.

After just a few moments of consideration, however, I suddenly realized the one thing in my life that I would change if I indeed had the chance. Needing no more time to think about this question, I answered that there is only one thing in my life I would change. I declared that I would go work in my grandmother's yard just one more time. Now, you may (as my questioner did) consider that a strange wish, but I felt strongly that my life would have more meaning if I could simply help my tiny, fragile grandmother plant green beans one more time.

For you see, I would no longer help her around the house because my father made me. I would gladly volunteer to help her and spend time with her because of how it made her feel. My grandmother loved her garden, and wanted her creation (those flowers and vegetables) to be perfect and beautiful. Also, I thought back on how happy she was to have my assistance and how much she enjoyed making my lunch. I recalled the stories she would share with me about growing up in the 1920s, about my family heritage, and about her experiences during her 84 years on this earth. Instead of a burdensome chore, I now remembered the yard work as the greatest of all experiences— simple, quality, family time.

Later I realized that my relationship with the Lord Jesus Christ is much like the time I spent with MawMaw. You see, we should not serve God because somebody makes us, or because we feel we must. Instead, we ought to serve God because we know it makes Him happy and because He wants His creation (you and me) to be perfect. We ought to long for intimate conversations with our Heavenly Father, as I now long for conversations with my grandmother.

If I could change anything, I would work in my grandmother's yard just one more time. But, you know, I will never again help MawMaw pull weeds and plant green beans and tomatoes. I will, however, be able to serve God in the future and volunteer to help Him make His creation, our world, and the people in it, perfect and without defect.

We all must understand that we have been called to live for Christ and may we "offer to God an acceptable service with reverence and awe" (**Hebrews 12:28**). I can't spend any more time with my grandmother, but I desire to spend more time with my God. This time, however, my father does not have to force me—I know the love of my Heavenly Father and want to share with Him quality time like I shared with MawMaw.

Whose Side Are You On?

One of history's most fascinating stories involves several Japanese soldiers from World War II who, even though the war ended in 1945, continued to fight the battle until the mid–1970s. These men were fighting a war they had already lost, a war they could never win, a war their country had already ended. These soldiers, ever faithful to the Imperial Army of Japan, refused to give up because they felt that the announcements of defeat were a trick by their enemy to convince them to surrender.

Shoichi Yokoi, a sergeant in the Japanese Imperial Army, gained international fame upon his return to Japan in 1972 for his dramatic tale of survival in the jungles of Guam for 27 years after the end of World War II. The Japanese public and media were intrigued by his bare diet of nuts, berries, frogs, snails and rats, and how he wove materials and clothing from tree bark.

Hiroo Onoda, a Japanese officer, kept a functioning weapon and was accused of killing several villagers before he was discovered in the Philippine jungle in 1974. According to press accounts, the Japanese military sent

Lieutenant Onoda to Lubang in 1944 with orders to spy on United States' forces. When more U.S. troops arrived at the end of the war, Onoda defiantly decided to stay, refusing to believe Japan really had given up. For decades after the war ended, he survived on food gathered from the jungle or stolen from local farmers. Onoda finally came out of hiding on March 10, 1975, after his former commanding officer traveled to Lubang to meet with him and convinced him to stop fighting.

The Bible explains that the things of God are foolishness to the person who does not know Christ as Savior. In **1 Corinthians 2:14**, Paul explains, "But people who aren't Christians can't understand these truths from God's Spirit. It all sounds foolish to them because only those who have the Spirit can understand what the Spirit means." Just like the Japanese men who would not listen to the calls for surrender, many people in our world refuse to surrender to Christ because they are still aligned with His enemy. They are still convinced of the glory of their cause, fighting valiantly for an army that will never win.

What makes this historical narrative even more interesting is the fact that other former Japanese soldiers, who had already surrendered and stopped fighting many years before, traveled to these remote villages and tried to convince their former comrades to lay down their arms, to give up the fight. Sadly, these stubborn soldiers, committed to a losing cause, would not listen, even to their fellow soldiers.

Our job as believers is to go find our former comrades, people who are still separated from Christ, and ask them to surrender. We who have left the losing side of sin and joined the winning side of the Savior need to search out those who have not been told that the war is over. We must explain to our still warring friends and family members that they have no chance of winning unless they join the winning side, the side aligned with the Almighty God and Judge, God the Father.

However, some of us need to stop fighting against Christ and give our lives to Him. Eternal life follows surrender, winning comes by leaving the losing side. If we know Jesus as Lord, we need to search out our lost comrades and tell them the truth. If we don't yet know Jesus, we must give our own lives to Him before we can help save others.

Whose side are you on? Have you given your life to the Father? Have you surrendered to Christ, or are you still fighting your own battles, hoping that you might win this war? Just like the Japanese soldiers, you and I have no chance of winning this spiritual battle because one side has already won. We simply must choose whether to fight vainly for the losers or surrender unconditionally to the winner. It is our choice.

Will you be like the rich young ruler who, when confronted with a similar choice, rejected Jesus and "went away grieving?" (**Matthew 19:22**) Or, will you be like Joshua, who proudly proclaimed, "choose for yourselves today whom you will serve...but as for me and my house, we will serve the Lord." (**Joshua 24:15**) What do you choose?

History in
the Making

How big does an event have to be to shape history? How long must an episode last for its effect to be felt forever?

On March 6, 1836, arguably the single most important and memorable event in Texas history took place. After this day, my state was never the same. No one who is alive today was in attendance then, yet we still feel its effects. Do you remember what happened that day 166 years ago?

On that day in the spring of 1836, in the small frontier town of San Antonio, 189 Texan heroes defended a small Catholic mission called the Alamo. Despite uncommon bravery and remarkable heroism, these soldiers lost the battle to Santa Anna and his Mexican army. Led by legendary men like James Bowie, William Travis, and Davy Crockett, these men gave their lives to see their dream accomplished. They volunteered to fight for Texas because they were convinced their cause, the cause of independence, was worth dying for.

Would it amaze you to learn that this most famous of Texas historical events, the crowning glory of Texan lore for over one and a half centuries, actually lasted for less than 90 minutes? Yes, that is true. The Mexican army laid siege to the Alamo for 13 days, but the final engagement took place on Sunday, March 6, 1836. This final battle, which lasted less than 2 hours, has come to symbolize what it means to be a Texan. So, how can such a short event in duration have such a profound impact on those who live so long afterward? Because men willingly gave their lives to see their cause, the dream of freedom and independence, accomplished.

There is another event in human history that lasted for just a short time but has seen its effects last forever. On that very first Easter weekend, in about 30 AD, a poor Jewish carpenter was executed because He stood up for what He believed. In a period described by Max Lucado as "Six Hours One Friday," thousands of years of human history, in fact, all of eternity, turned on a period of short duration. In a demonstration of courage and bravery that trumps the most valiant Alamo defender, Jesus of Nazareth died because He, too, believed His cause, God's cause, was worth fighting and dying for.

Just as Texans annually celebrate the Battle of the Alamo and remember the bravery of its defenders, Christians gather annually to remember the sacrificial death of their hero, the Messiah. One dramatic difference, however, exists between the soldiers of San Antonio and Jesus Christ, the carpenter turned evangelist.

After the battle ended and the fighting stopped, the men of the Alamo were buried and seen no more, for they died as merely heroic humans, never to live again. When Jesus died and was buried after His battle on that first Good Friday, He rose again three days later on that first Easter Sunday. The defeat by the brave Texan soldiers was followed by death; Jesus' apparent defeat was followed by the glory of His miraculous resurrection.

It is said that William Barret Travis, a twenty-six year old cavalry officer, drew a line in the dirt of the mission and asked men to cross over to his side if they were filling to fight and defend the Alamo.

Today, Jesus Christ is asking people from all over Texas, from all over the world, to cross the line of selfishness and pride to join His side, to commit their lives to Him.

Jesus lives today, calling people, even Texans, to join His victorious army, to celebrate His victory over sin and death, to give their lives to the service of the ultimate hero. While defending the Alamo, Travis wrote those famous words, "Victory or Death." Sadly, soon after writing this, Travis faced death and failed to achieve victory. At the cross of Calvary, however Jesus earned spiritual victory for you and me by His death and resurrection.

Can one event short in time have a lasting effect? It can if God the Father calls God the Son to fight and win a battle that men and women can never win alone. What is that event? It is our source of eternal hope, the reason we say today "Happy Easter."

Are You Hot or Cold?

When was the last time you had your temperature taken? Physicians check our body temperatures to determine our health. If one's body gets too hot or too cold, a medical problem exists. Therefore, in the medical field, luke-warmness is beneficial. However, in the spiritual realm, nothing is more dangerous than that tempting middle ground between hot and cold known as lukewarmness.

In the book of Revelation, the Apostle John shares the words of Jesus with the churches of Asia Minor. In **Revelation chapter 3**, Jesus spoke His rebuke against the church in Laodicea. John quotes Jesus when he writes, "I know your deeds, that you are neither cold nor hot. I wish you were either one or the other! So, because you are lukewarm—neither hot nor cold—I am about to spit you out of my mouth."

As I studied this passage, I asked God to show me how to avoid being lukewarm. If Jesus hates tepidness so much, as believers we must prioritize its avoidance. Serving Christ requires one to serve the wishes of Christ, including His wish regarding our spiritual body temperature.

In my mind, there are three ways to become luke-warm, and therefore, three warnings for us as believers.

First, water becomes lukewarm if it has been sitting out for a while. What once was hot or cold has lost the extremeness of its temperature because it has not been heated or cooled in a long time. In a sense, the water left alone for long periods of time sees its temperature extremes simply fade away.

Do you know that Christians also lose their extremeness, their fervor, their passion, their energy when they have been sitting still for a while? There are people in all of our churches who formerly were active, serving members but no longer demonstrate that excitement and fervor. As Christian leaders, we need to find these formerly active believers and get them excited again, restore their energy and help them get off the spiritual bench.

Second, water becomes lukewarm if you try to mix hot and cold together. Interestingly, if you mix a lot of hot and a lot of cold, you get lukewarm. Conversely, if you mix a little hot and a little cold, you still get lukewarm. No matter the formula, the result of mixing hot and cold together is lukewarmness.

Sadly, many Christian believers try to mix hot and cold and come up with hot. Some mix a lot of hot, a great deal of passion for God, with a lot of cold, a life of habitual sin. This person ends up lukewarm. Other believers don't really possess much that is hot, nor do they involve themselves in much that is cold. They simply put their little bit of hot and their little bit of cold together and end up lukewarm. Either way, the result of mixing hot and cold is neither one.

Third, cold water becomes lukewarm when it is around hot water. Conversely, hot water becomes lukewarm when it is around cold water. If you put a cup of cold water on the stove, it will warm up. If you put warm water in the refrigerator, it will lose its heat. Therefore, the environment surrounding the water affects its temperature.

As Christians, we must never forget that we are to be influencers in this world, not influencees. Jesus called us to make a difference, to be salt and light in a dark world. We will lose our hotness if we spend too much time in and around the cold world of sin. We are never to leave the world, but we are also never to love the world. Let's not lose our spiritual hotness because we got caught up with the world's coldness.

Jesus hates lukewarmness. Of that there is no debate. So, how do we avoid this medium point on the spiritual thermometer? How does one get to be lukewarm? How does the heat dissipate?

We must remember that hot water becomes luke-warm when it is forgotten and ignored. When left alone, hot or cold water loses its hotness or coldness. So does your passion for Jesus Christ dissipate when it is forgotten and ignored. If you feel lukewarm, ask God to demon-strate to you the ways in which you have forgotten Him.

In **Hosea 4:6**, we read about the dangers of luke-warmness. Stating His divine hatred for this medium spiritual temperature, God said, "My people are destroyed for lack of knowledge. Because you have rejected knowl-edge, I also will reject you from being My priest. Since you have forgotten the law of your God, I also will forget your children."

Conversely, in **Jeremiah 50:4–5**, we read about the people of Judah who returned to God and became spiritu-ally hot again. "It will be the Lord their God they will seek. They will ask for the way to Zion, turning their faces in its direction; they will come that they may join themselves to the Lord in an everlasting covenant that will not be forgotten."

These two Old Testament passages indicate two im-portant truths. One, it is frighteningly easy to become spiritually cold. We must be diligent and vigilant to avoid losing our heat. But, secondly, the passage in Jeremiah's prophecy encourages us that we can return to the land of hotness, if we do as they did. How did they get hot again? They turned their face in God's direction and joined themselves to the Lord.

In the 14th Century, Johannes Tauler wrote, "It is no longer the fashion to suffer for the sake of God, and to bear the Cross for Him; for the diligence and real earnestness, that perchance were found in man, have been extinguished and have grown cold; and now no one is willing any longer to suffer distress for the sake of God."

In our day, 700 years later, we must ask ourselves if we have grown cold or are we willing to suffer distress for the sake of God. Am I still on fire for Christ, or has my hotness faded into lukewarmness? What about you? What is your spiritual temperature?

May we always be hot for Him.

The Prayers of a Hurting Nation

September 11, 2001 is a day Americans will never forget. The tragic attack on New York City and Washington, D.C. by cowards who call themselves zealots will have many effects on our nation. We are already seeing many of them: increased airport security, racial and religious prejudice committed against some people, amazing acts of kindness and love provided by others, heroic rescue attempts accomplished by firefighters of all races and religions. However, I believe the greatest effects of this event on our nation will be a renewed spiritual appetite among Americans, a true sense of revival, and a renewed call to prayer.

When tragedy strikes, the most fundamental human questions arise. "Why did this happen?" "Why could God allow all those people to die?" I know the questions exist, but sadly, sometimes our only answers are "I'm not sure. Let's just hold on." and "Remember, our Heavenly Father truly loves us." Those answers may seem shallow and incomplete, but they are built on the foundation of true faith.

True faith is demonstrated by those who trust even when they don't understand. True faith is expressed when people cry out to God for answers, and then trust Him, even when the answers don't come as quickly as we would like. True faith believes what the writer of Hebrews wrote. "Faith is the assurance of things hoped for, the conviction of things not seen." We have not yet seen all the results of this tragedy, but our God is the God of hope.

I know that many of you attended prayer services on that Tuesday evening at your churches; we held one at ours. In many places across our land, people offered prayers in response to this tragedy. They offered prayers of thanks, prayers of sorrow, prayers of desperation, prayers of mourning, and prayers of repentance. In one location near our church, people were allowed to write their prayers.

I had the privilege of reading some of these prayers and observing the great faith displayed by my neighbors. After reading them, I could not wait to share them with others. These prayers, prayed to their God in a quiet room, in a private moment, will strengthen your faith. These prayers, spoken, not to gain public notoriety, but to work through tragic fears, will remind us that our God reigns. These prayers, written in English, Spanish, and even Arabic, remind us that prayer comforts and heals. May I share a few of them with you?

- One woman wrote, "*Lord, we don't have answers today, but we know that you are in control. Please keep us mindful of your grace and protection. May we always look to you for answers and strength.*"

- A humble gentleman prayed, "*Dear God, thank You for my sister's illness today that kept her from her job as a flight attendant. I pray for all those who lost loved ones today. I pray for our President and all those making decisions for our country. Keep us steadfast in our faith, looking to you for strength. Amen.*"

- Another woman asked, "*Lord, if we could really see this from Your perspective, wouldn't we rejoice? Not at the loss of life, but at what great good must come out of such terrible evil. Help us to get hold of that and believe. May Your presence, and direction, and love, and power really dwell in us now, more than our own weakness. We do love You. Help us as a people to love You and love each other more— even perfectly. All praise to You.*"

- A child wrote, "*Heavenly Father, please be with those who are suffering so. Please be with those who are trying to clean the rubble and find bodies. Please, Lord, be with us as a nation wounded. With your help, Lord, we will get through this.*"

- Finally, one woman who must really trust God asked "*for peace in the knowledge that You, Lord, are in control. For the wisdom and courage to live out what You would have us to do in extraordinary times. In thanksgiving for those You kept safe. For the divine comfort for all those who have lost loved ones and/or a way of life. For Your wisdom, grace, and power over President Bush and our many leaders. You are still on the throne and good. Bring many, many to You through this. Amen.*"

To the original authors of these prayers: Please forgive us for entering your private sanctuary. But, thank you for writing them, and thank you for letting us read them. Your faith is too strong and your words are too eloquent not to be shared with others. Your prayers and your trust in our God help us heal. Thank you.

To the readers of these prayers: Take these words of hope and add them to your own. Our world is full of evil people, but our world is ruled by a sovereign God. Your reaction to this tragedy can either pull you toward Him or push you away. My prayer is that you will be drawn to a greater faith than ever before. I believe the authors of these silent prayers have already been drawn to Him. Will you join us at His throne?

God bless America.

Whom Will You Serve?

During the American Civil War, many notable families faced the struggle of having male family members fight on opposing sides of the conflict. During this war, many people faced the difficult decision of choosing whether to support their homelands or their relatives. Some Americans eventually chose to protect states' rights or slavery or industry rather than remain committed to their family members.

Flora Cooke, the daughter of Union general Philip Saint George Cooke, married James Ewell Brown (JEB) Stuart, a West Point graduate and courageous Confederate cavalry general from Virginia. John Rogers Cooke, Flora's brother, attended Harvard and became a U.S. Army infantry officer before choosing to side with the Confederacy during the Civil War.

So, Mrs. JEB Stuart faced the emotional dilemma of watching her husband and her brother fight for the South while her father commanded Northern troops. This decision weighed heavily on Flora's heart until, in 1861, she finally committed to supporting the South and her husband and brother, instead of the North and her father. She demonstrated the finality of this decision when she legally changed the name of her son who originally had been named in honor of his grandfather.

On at least two occasions, Gen. JEB Stuart and Gen. Philip Saint George Cooke fought on opposing sides in battle. Can you imagine the emotional struggle that Flora Cooke Stuart faced as she awaited the news reports that followed these conflicts?

Even the family of American President Abraham Lincoln faced this difficult and emotionally burdensome situation. As the Commander in Chief of the Union Army, he oversaw the military efforts of the Northern troops. In addition to his own role with the Union forces, Abraham Lincoln's son, Robert, served in the Union Army under General (and future President) Ulysses S. Grant.

Ironically, however, Mary Todd Lincoln, the wife of the President, had three stepbrothers and three brothers–in–law that fought for the Confederacy during the Civil War. All three stepbrothers were killed during the war. Mary Todd Lincoln's half–sister Emily Todd Helm was married to a Confederate general from Kentucky named Ben Hardin Helm who was killed during the Battle of Chicamagua in 1863.

Just as the members of these historically significant

families had to choose the cause of the North or the South over their devotion to relatives and friends, disciples of Jesus Christ much choose devotion to Him over finances, fame, and even family. In **Luke 14:26–27**, Jesus said, "If anyone comes to Me, and does not hate his own father and mother and wife and children and brothers and sisters, yes, and even his own life, he cannot be My disciple. Whoever does not carry his own cross and come after Me cannot be My disciple."

Most theologians agree that Jesus' emphasis was on the desire to be a disciple, not His apparent command to hate one's own relatives. The Messiah wanted His followers to be so closely connected to Him that every other relationship would pale in importance by comparison.

The authors of the Bible Knowledge Commentary explain these verses in this way. "To emphasize that discipleship is difficult, Jesus said that one must hate his own family and even his own life in order to be His disciple. Literally hating one's family would have been a violation of the Law. Since Jesus on several occasions admonished others to fulfill the Law, He must not have meant here that one should literally hate his family. The stress here is on the priority of love. One's loyalty to Jesus must come before his loyalty to his family or even to life itself."

Jesus wanted His disciples to understand that His cause, the devotion He expected of His followers, must take precedence over all other interests and issues. To be a fully devoted follower of Christ, we must place a lesser value on all other concerns and allegiances. The Messiah expected His earthly followers to recognize that commitment to Him meant that nothing else could ever be first priority again.

Just as some Americans in the 1860s had to choose allegiance to a cause over commitment to a family member, Christians today must choose to wholeheartedly devote themselves to the cause of Christ over family, money, prestige, comfort, or personal ambition.

John MacArthur wrote, "Salvation involves a commitment to forsake sin and to follow Jesus Christ at all costs. He will take disciples on no other terms."

To live out this complete devotion, we must commit to follow Christ as wholeheartedly as Joshua committed his life to the worship and service of Yahweh in the Old Testament. We must emulate Joshua's commitment and ask ourselves, "Choose for yourselves today whom you will serve, but as for me and my house, we will serve the LORD." **(Joshua 24:15)**

Have you given up all other allegiances and made Him Lord and Master of all? Are you ready to go to war for Christ?

About the Author

Trey Graham, M.Div., is a minister, writer, and speaker who specializes in the areas of Leadership, Vision Casting, and Goal Setting. Trey believes that God has called all people to be leaders, and that leaders are developed as they study the Word of God and apply God's principles to everyday life. He graduated from the United States Military Academy at West Point, and served as a U.S. Army Field Artillery officer prior to becoming a pastor. He is a true teacher and motivator who helps people set goals and achieve them.

Trey leads Faith Walk Ministries, which exists to teach Christians to become leaders of Godly character, and to encourage Christians to "walk by faith, not by sight." As a training and resource ministry, Faith Walk provides biblical teaching and leadership training gained from experience. Trey Graham believes that God has called him to share the biblical principles of success and leadership that can change lives, renew churches, and bring about much needed revival in the United States.

Faith Walk Ministries, founded as Trey's speaking and writing ministry, offers training programs in the areas of Christian Leadership, Vision Casting, and Goal Setting. Trey writes numerous columns for magazines and newspapers across the United States and Canada. Trey also frequently shares motivational and inspirational messages to audiences of all types at church conferences and retreats.

Trey and his wife Bretta live in Plano, Texas with their children.

For more information, or to schedule a leadership training seminar for your church or organization, please contact Faith Walk Ministries at:

www.faithwalkministries.com

From this website, you may also schedule Trey Graham as a speaker.